MANDALA DESIGN: COLORING BOOK FOR ADULTS

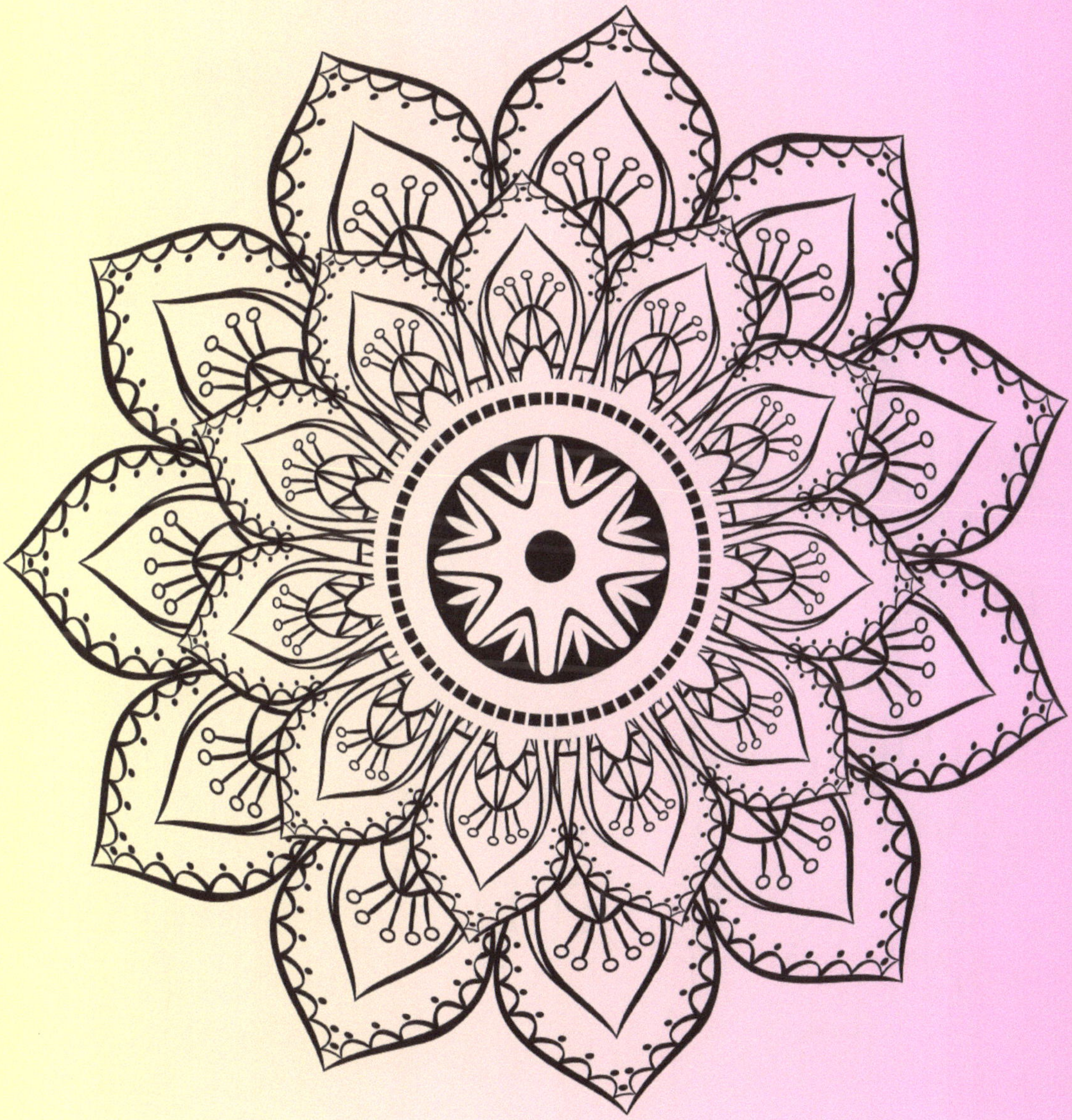

Our mandala design colouring book can help you to be creative and at calm. This colouring book has exquisitely intricate mandala patterns that are great for reducing stress and encouraging mindfulness. Each page has been printed on premium paper so you may colour with your preferred medium without worrying about bleed-through. This mandala design colouring book is the ideal companion for anyone looking to unwind and express their creativity, offering over 22 distinctive designs to pick from.

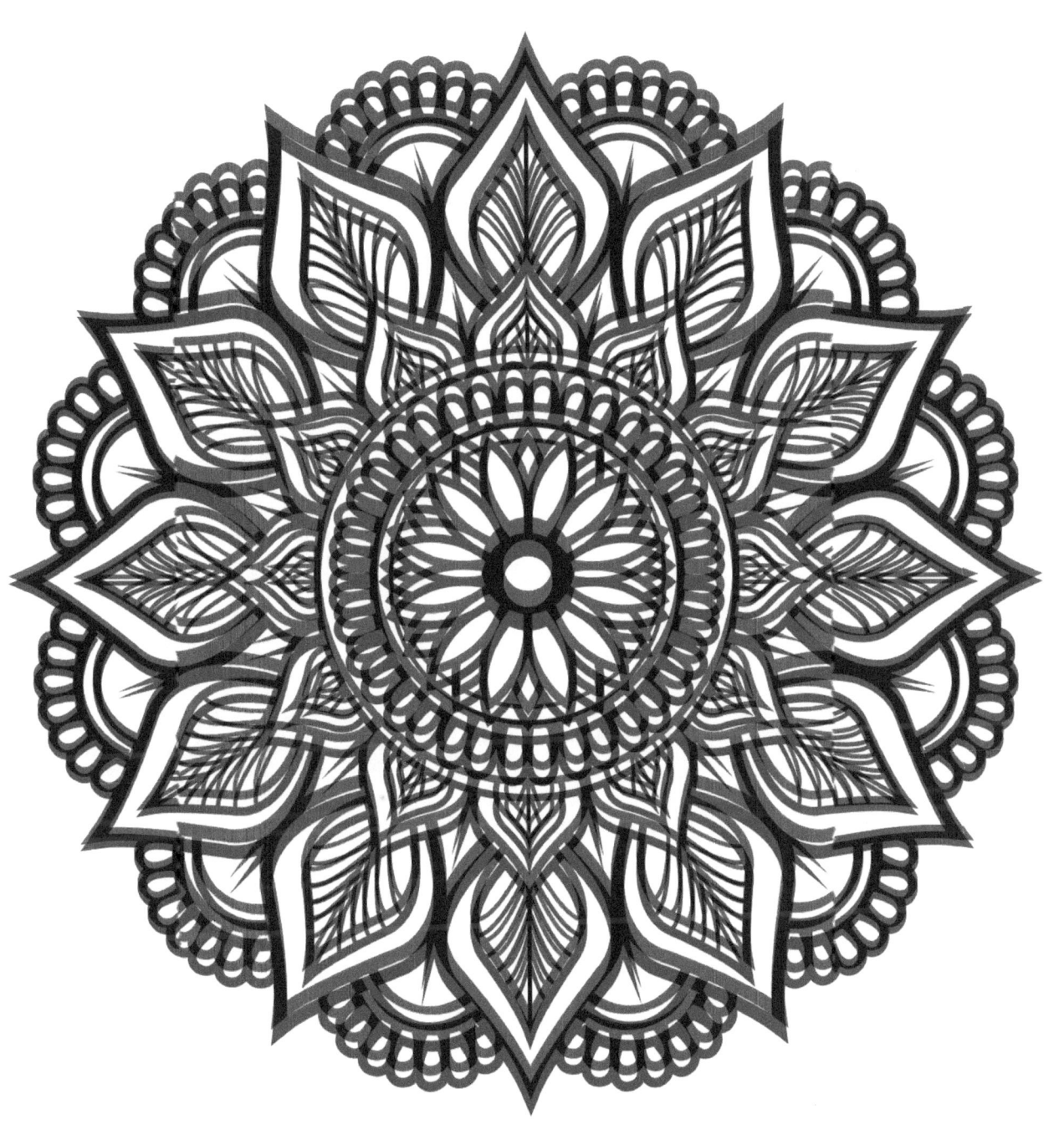

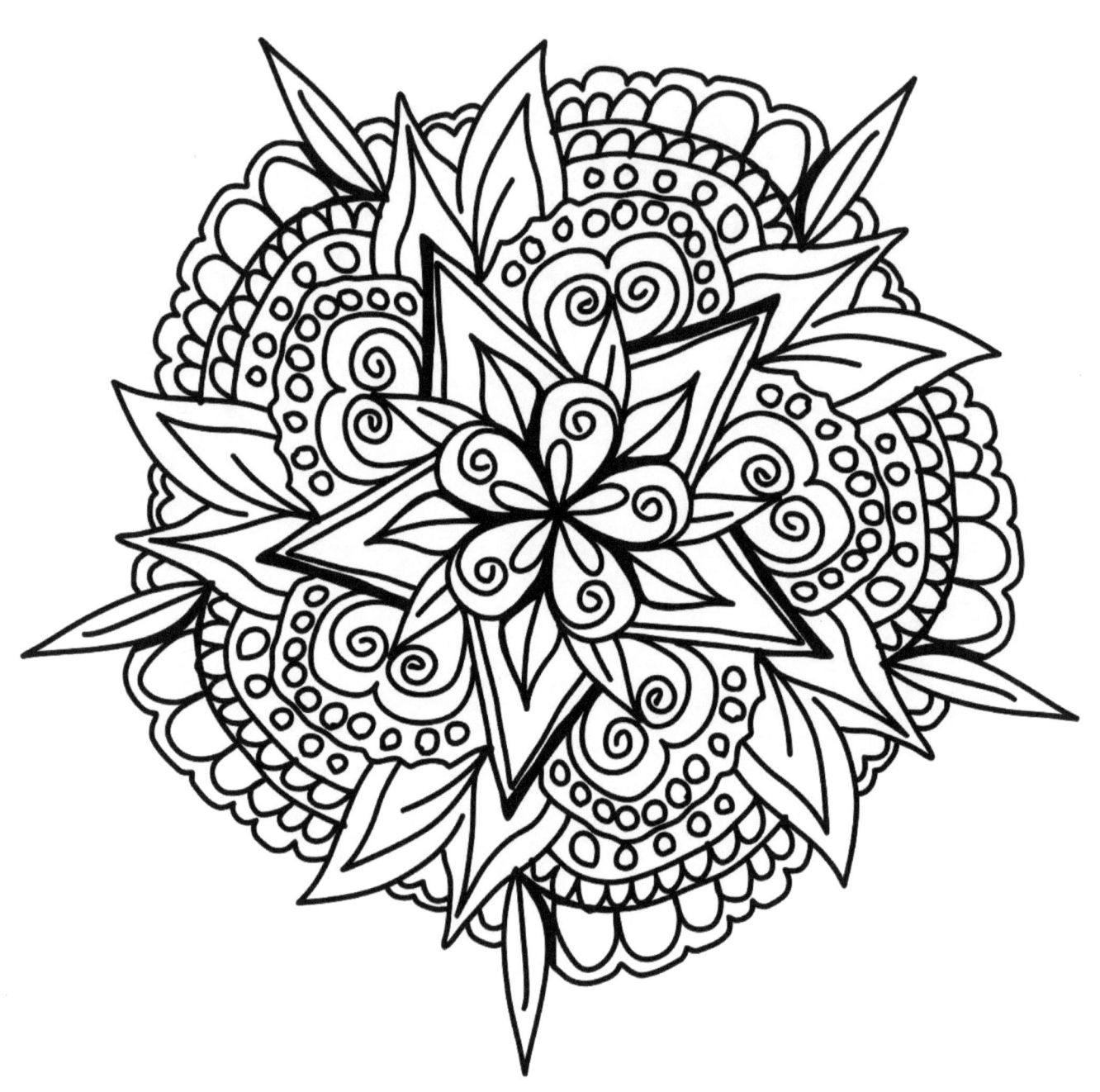

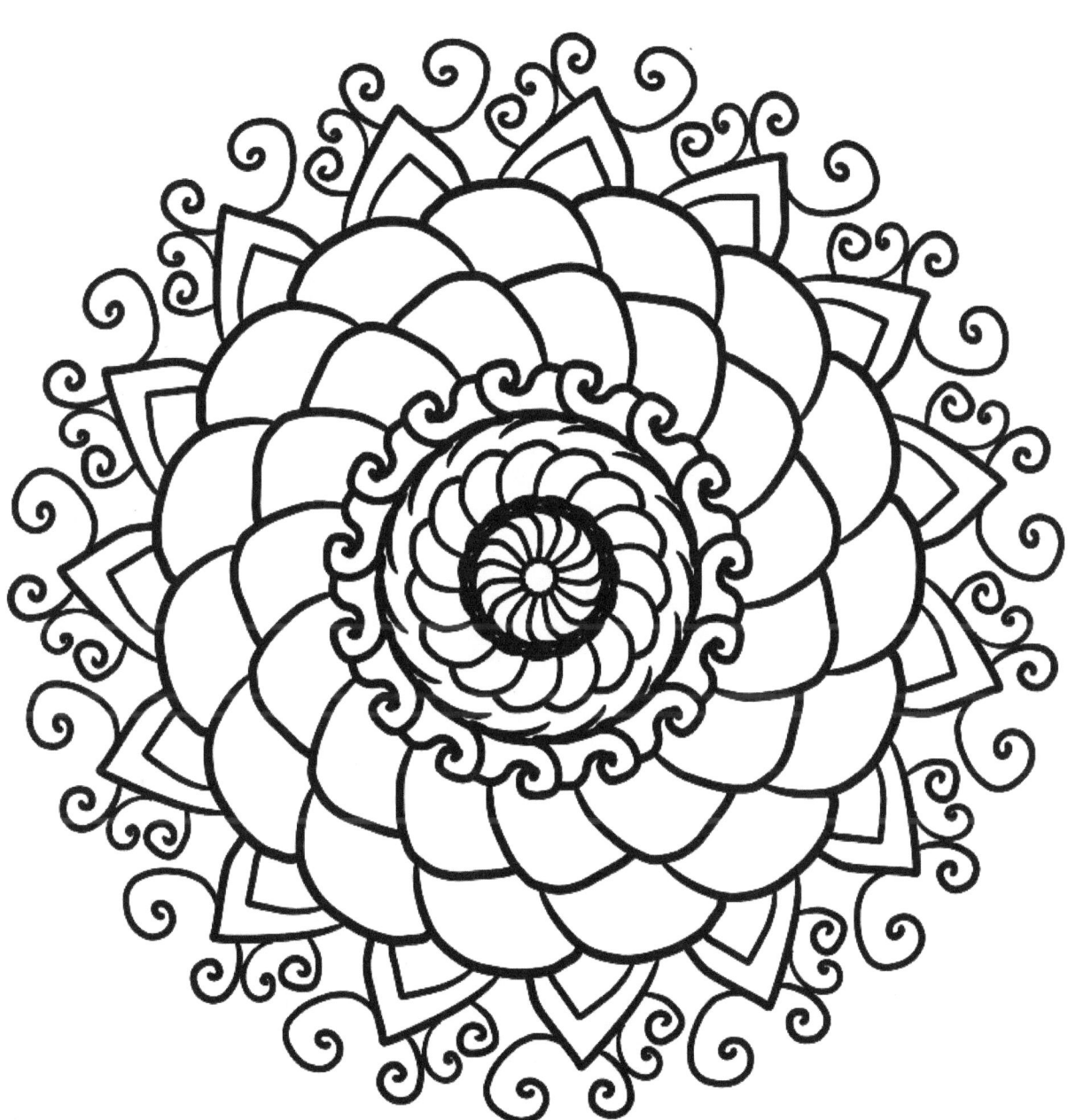

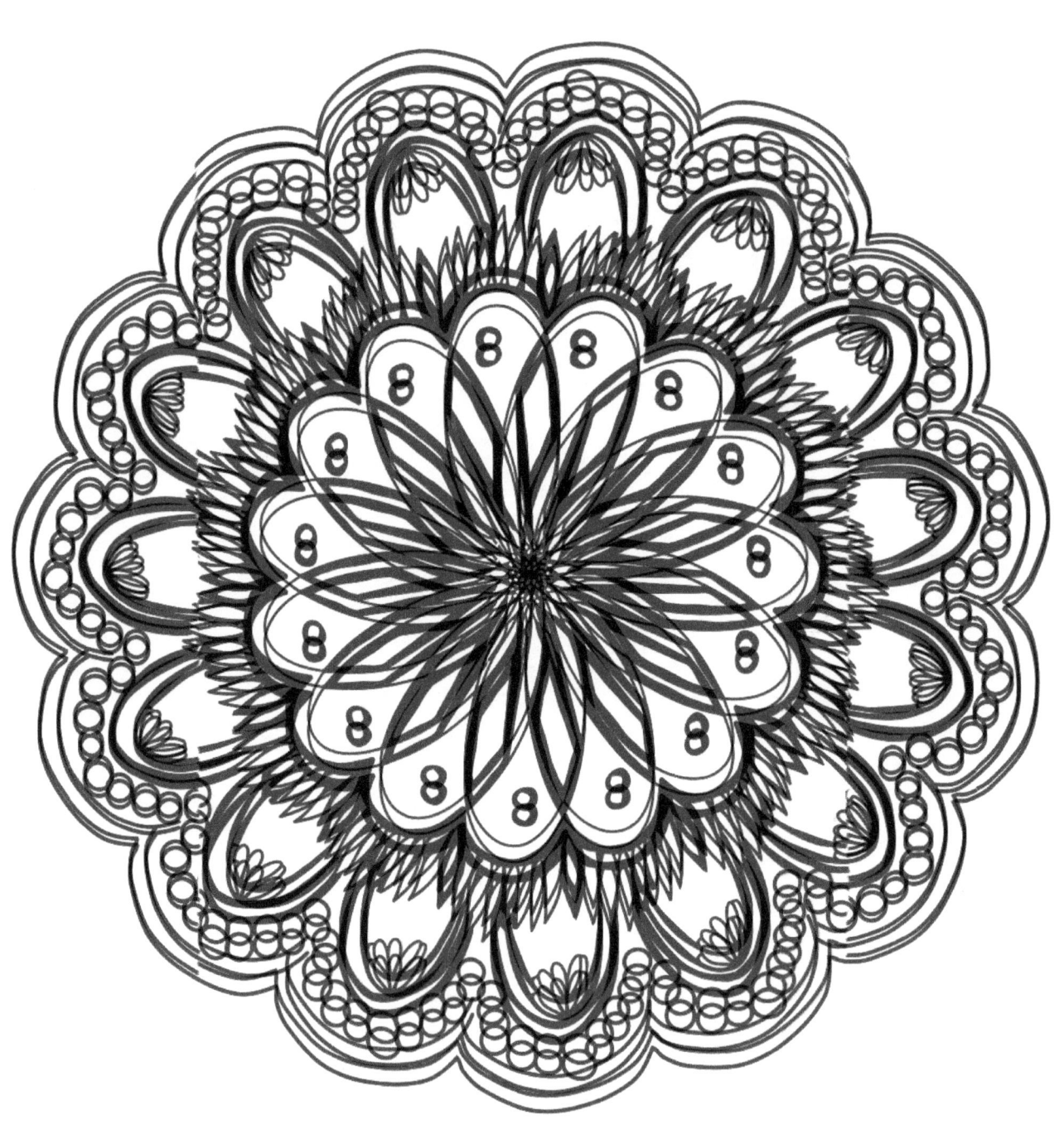

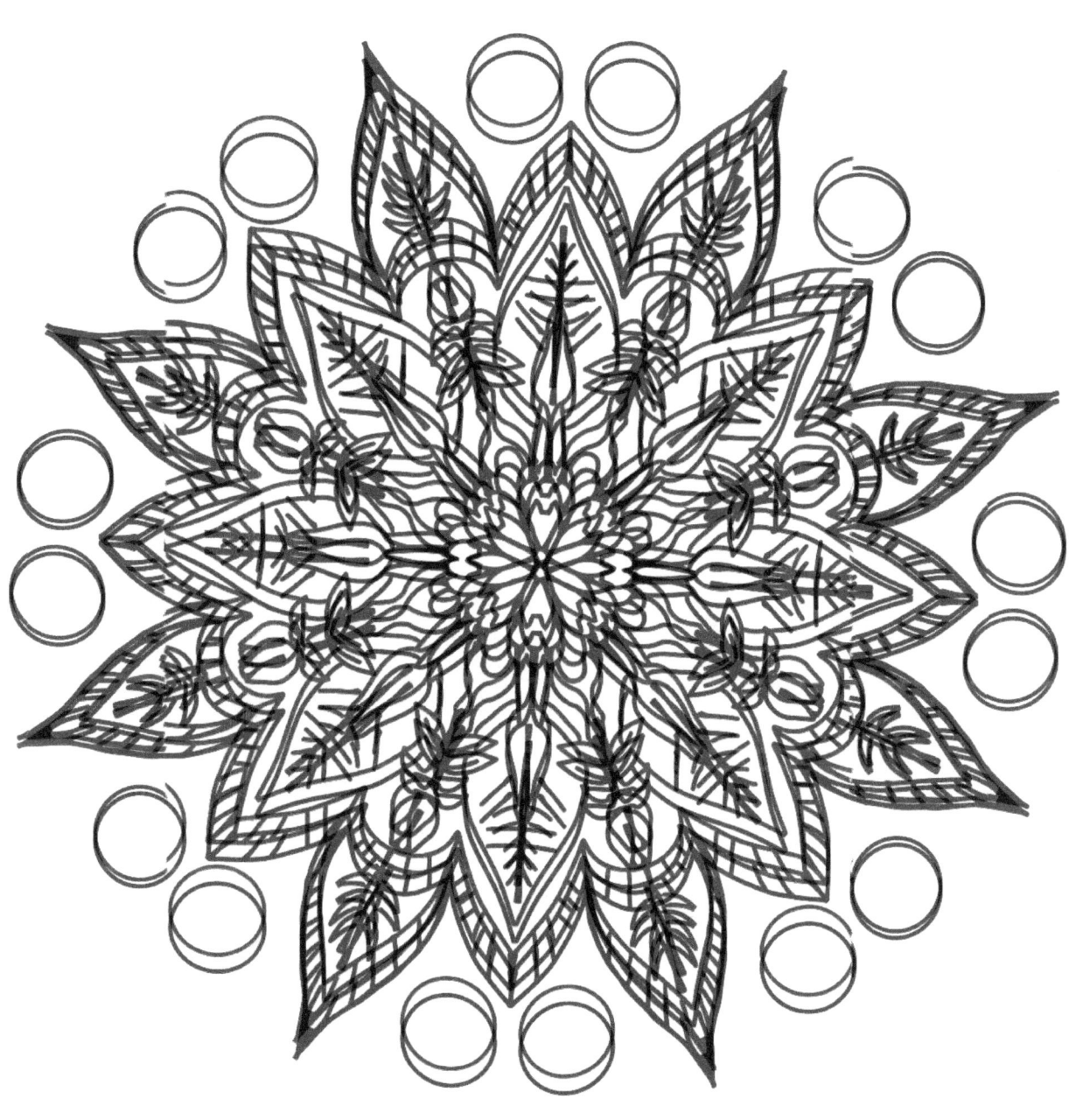

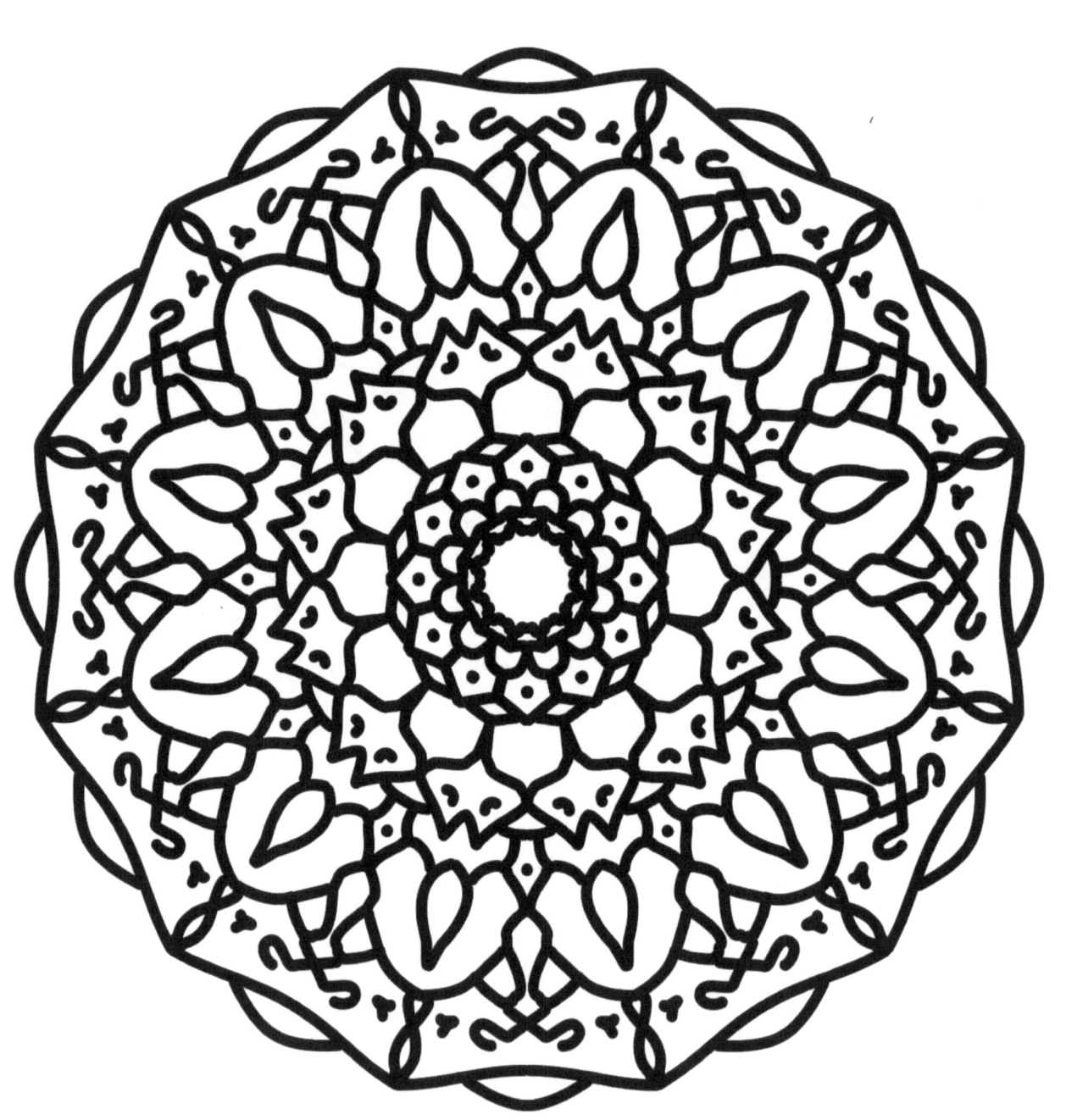

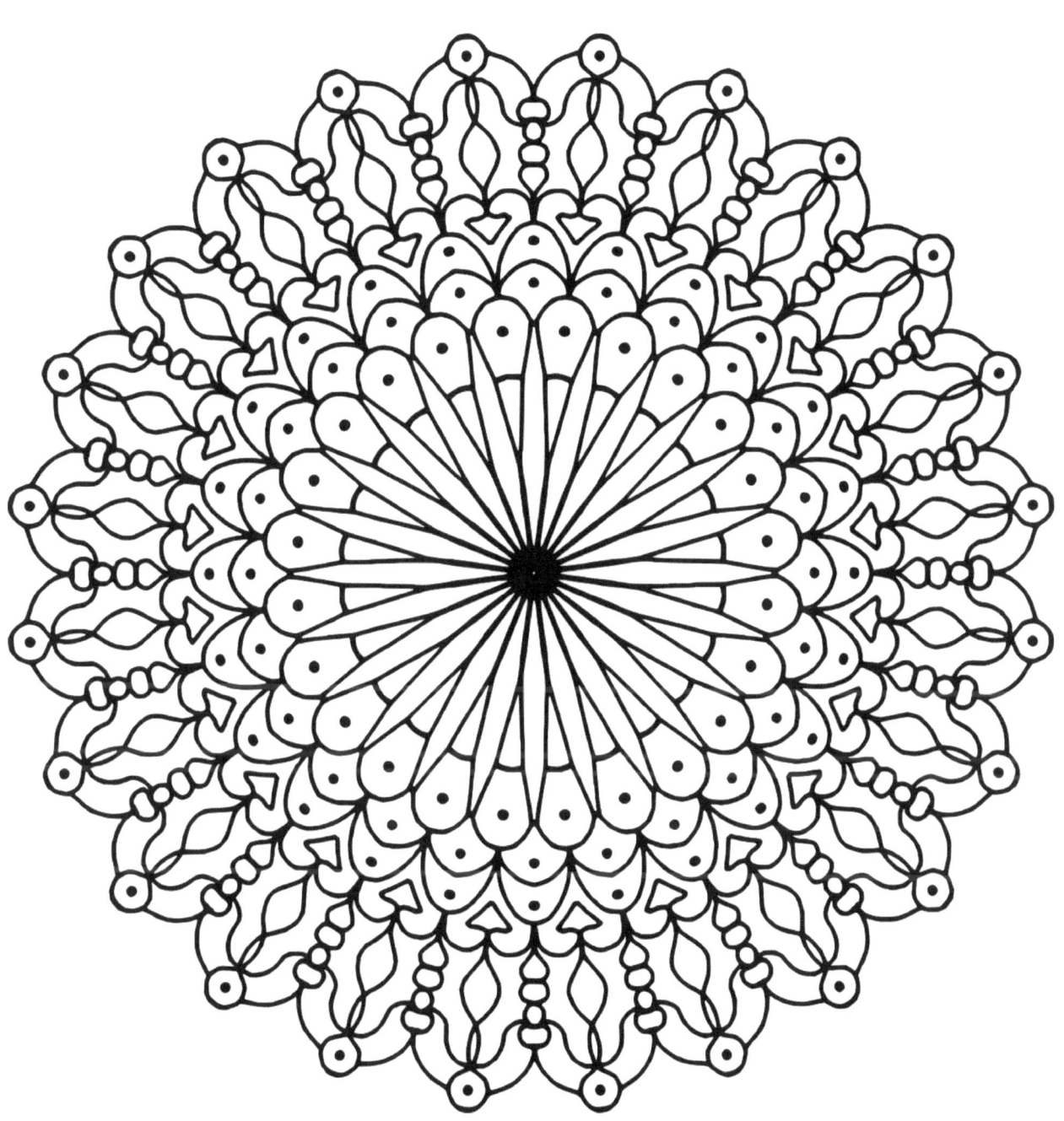

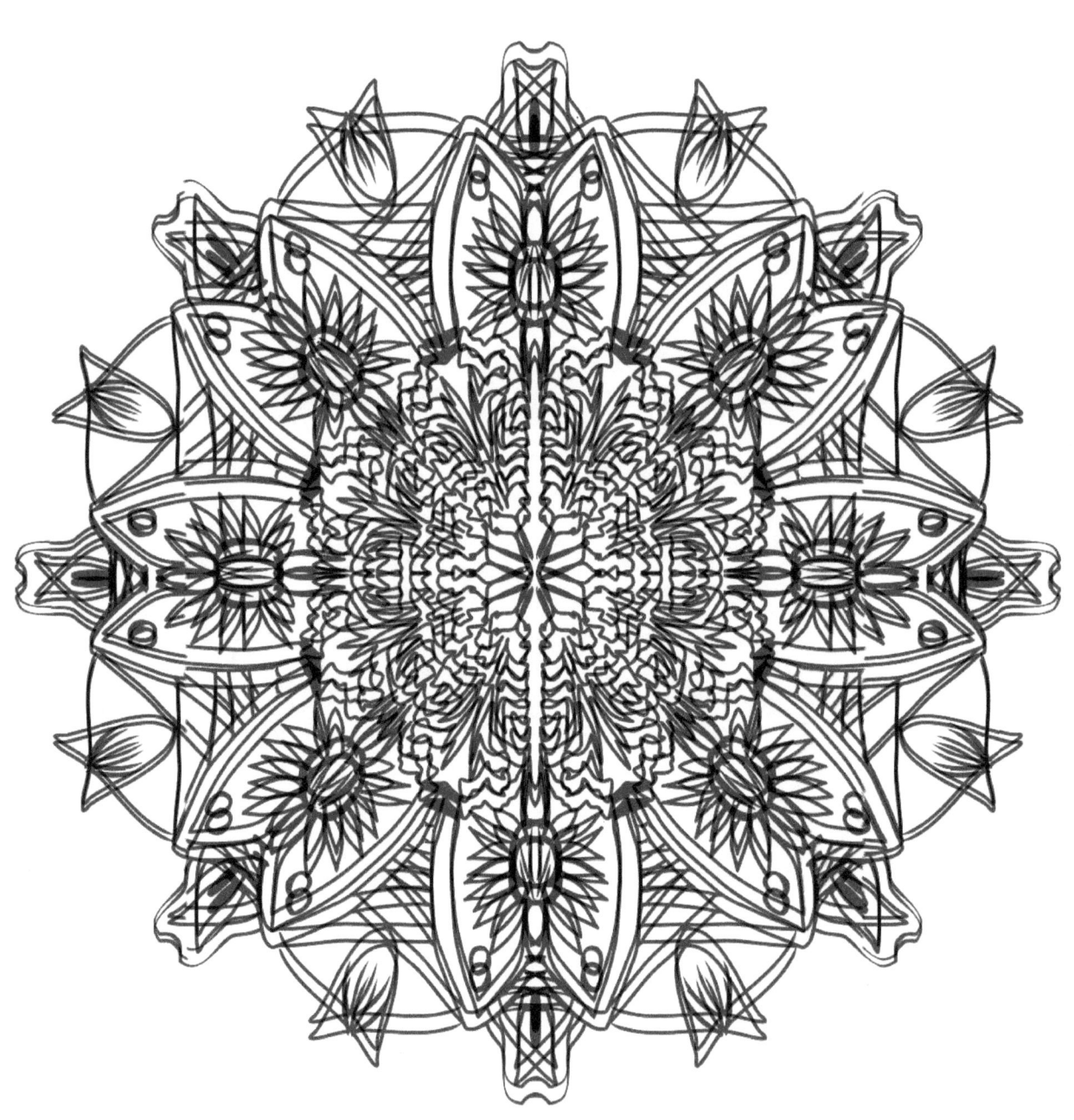

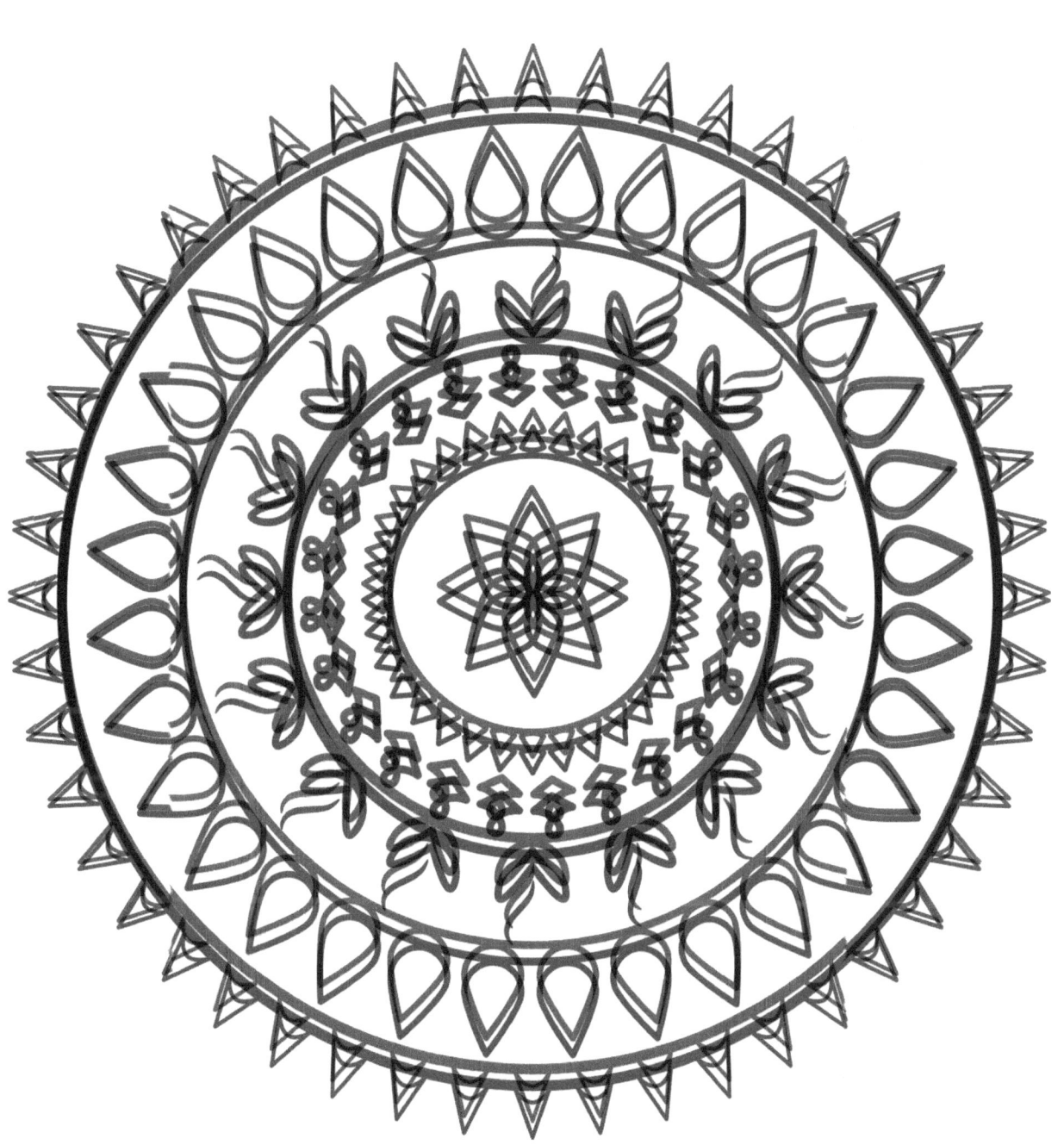

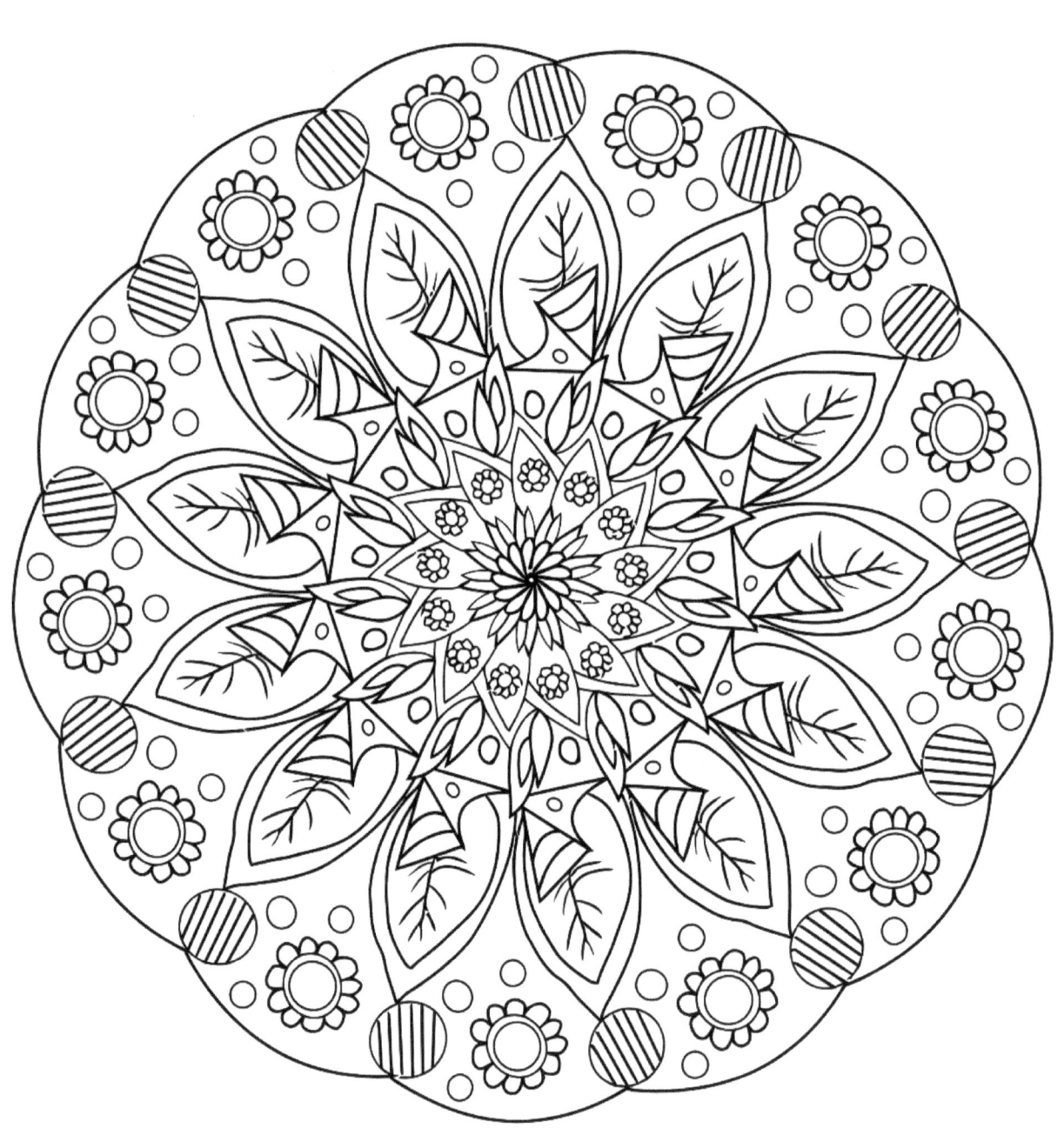

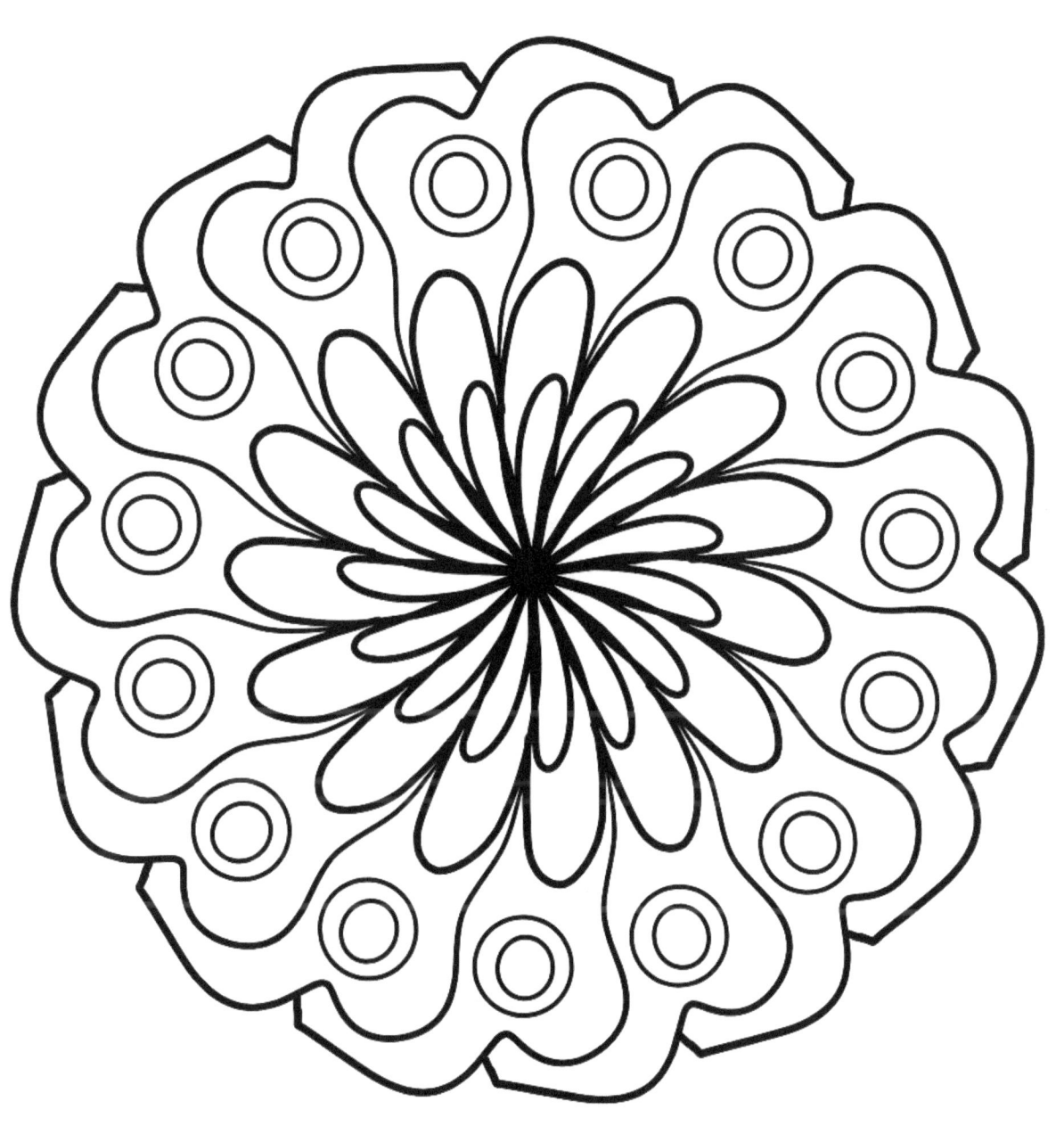

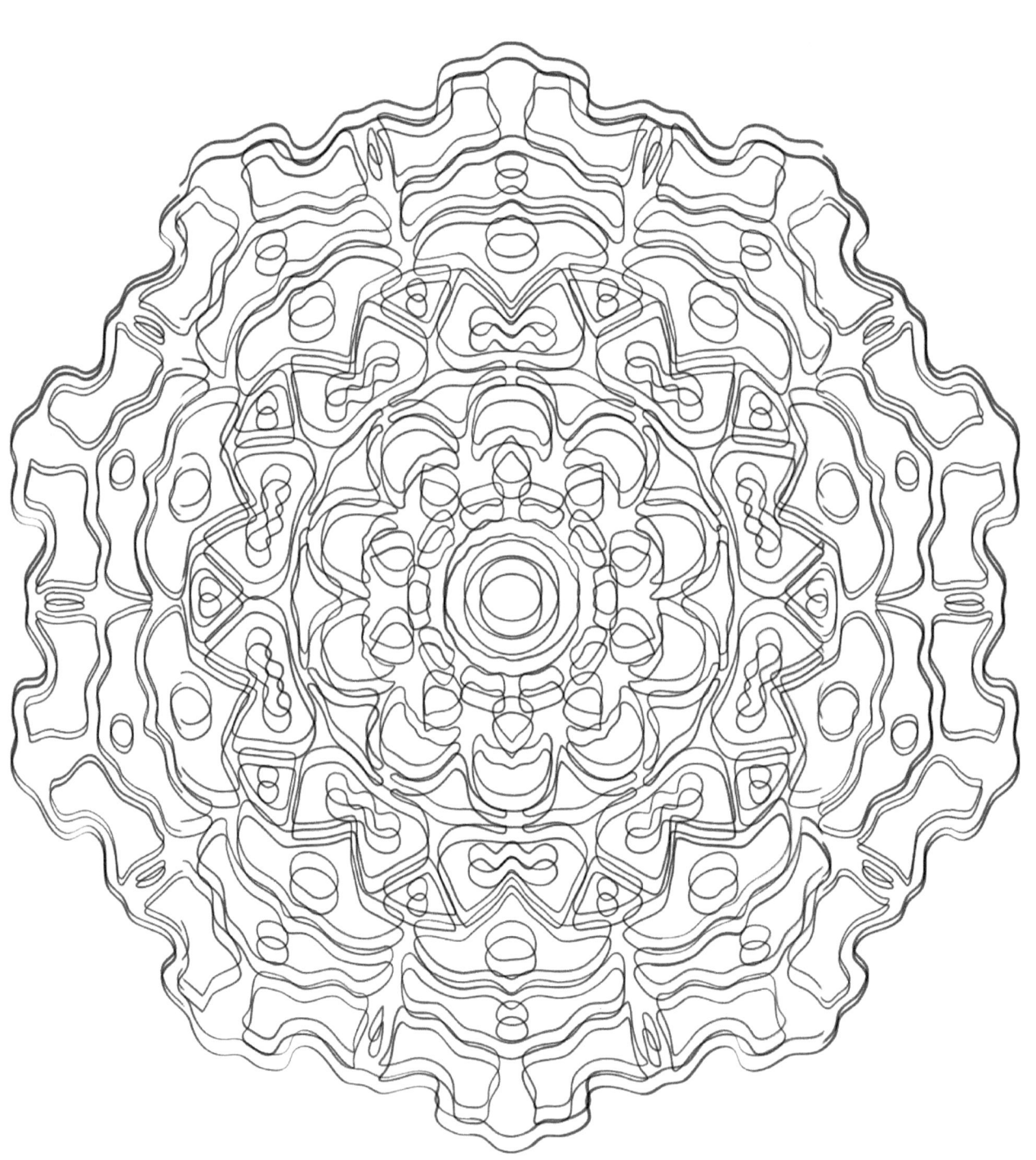

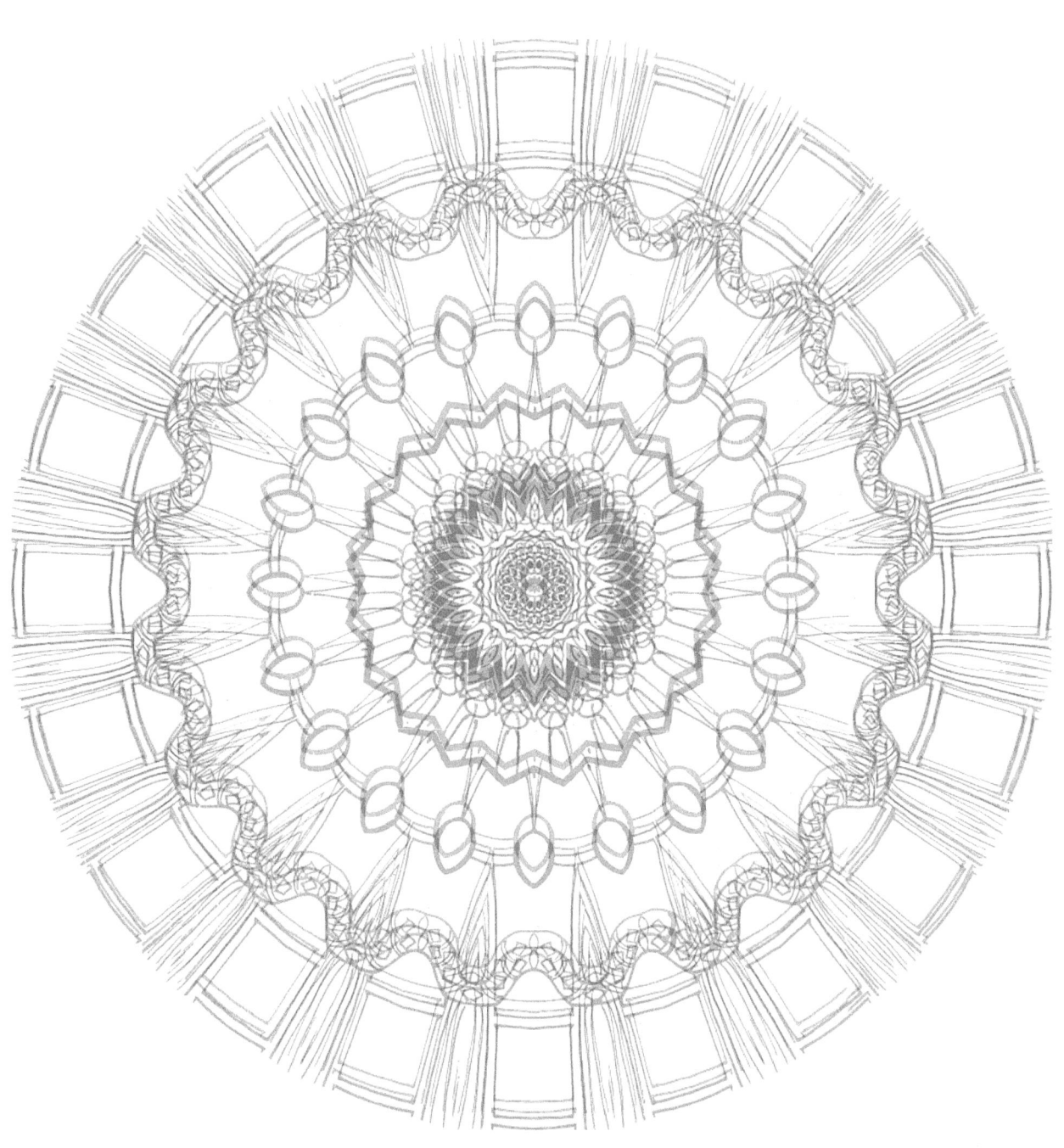

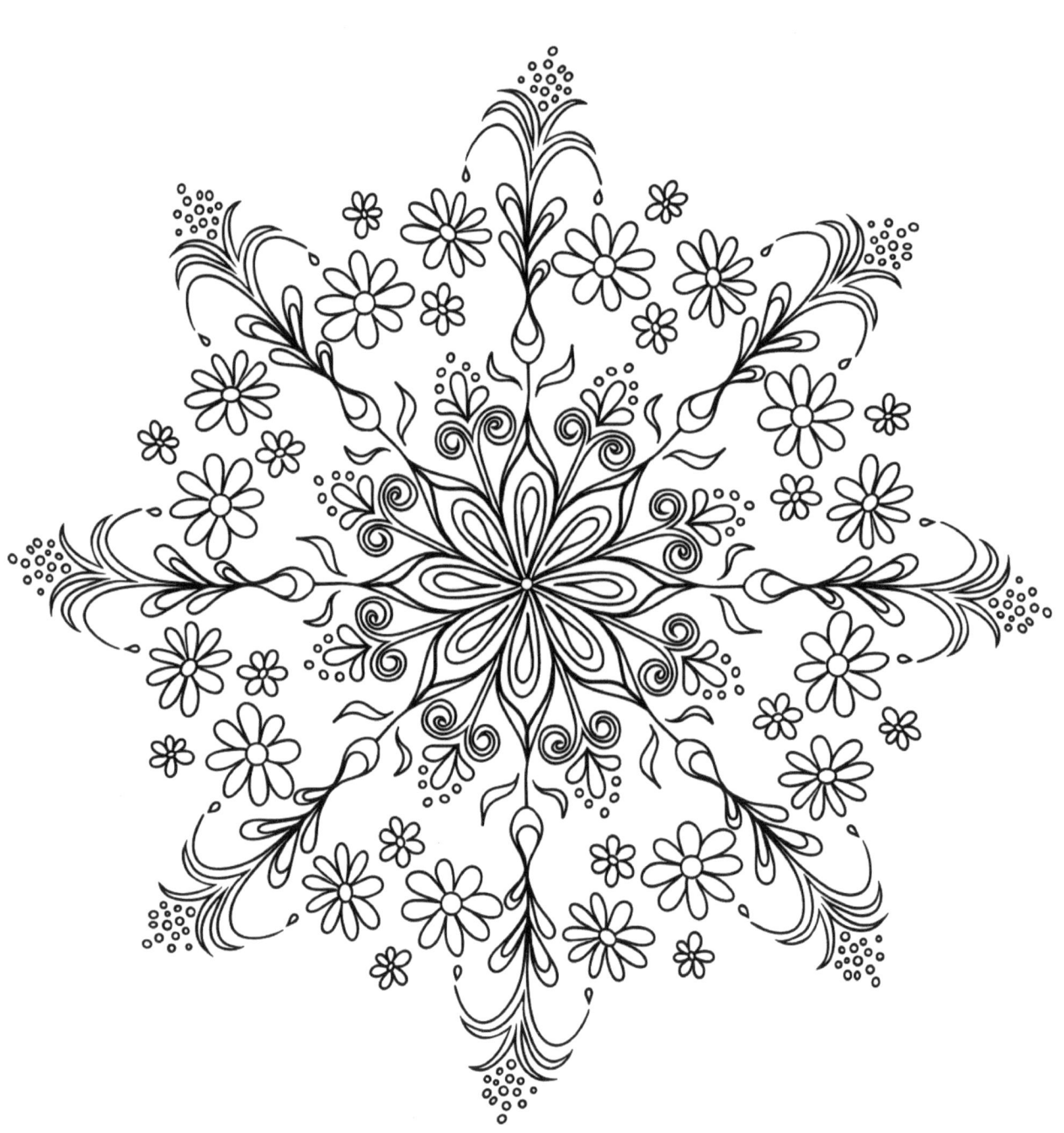

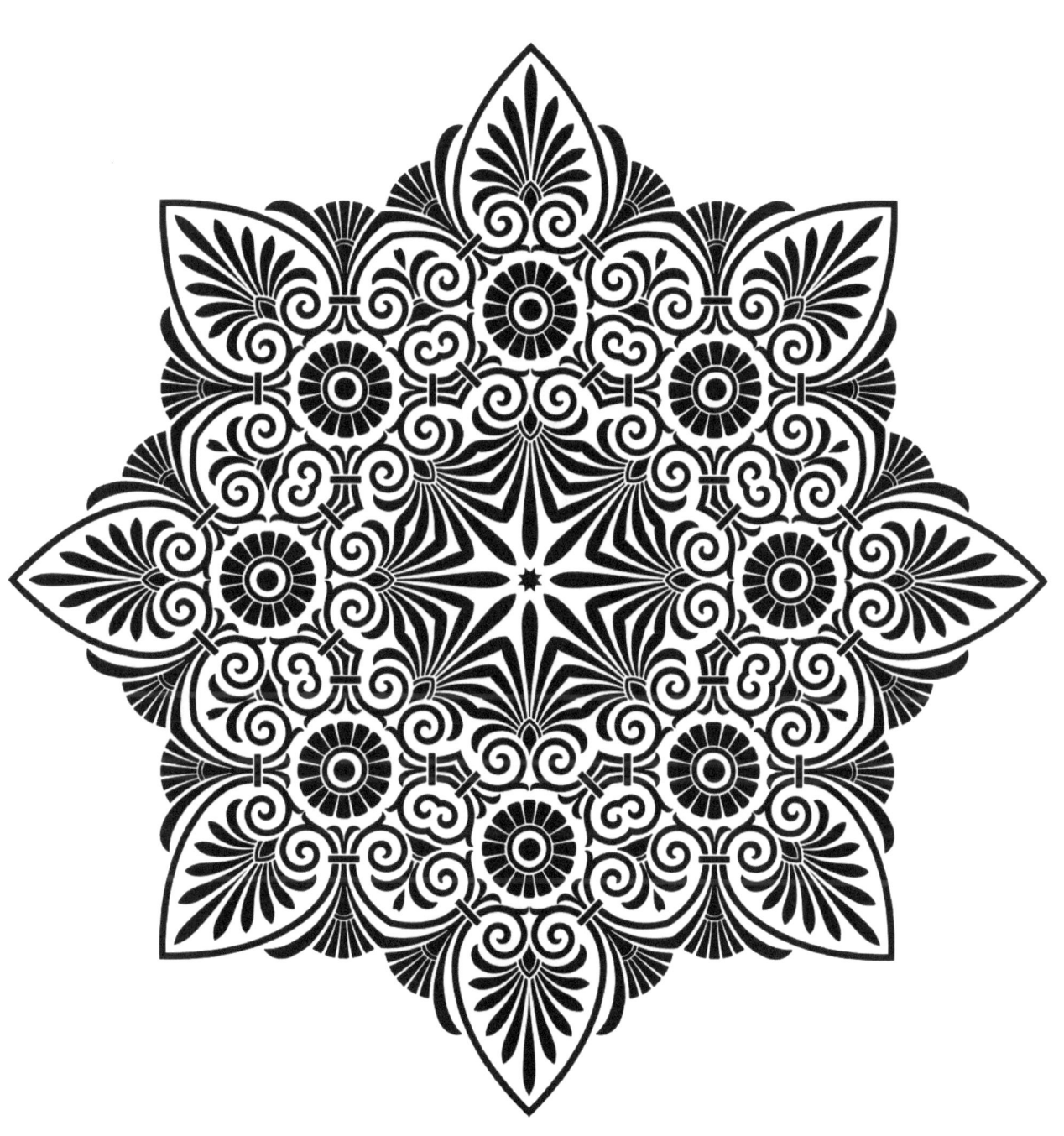

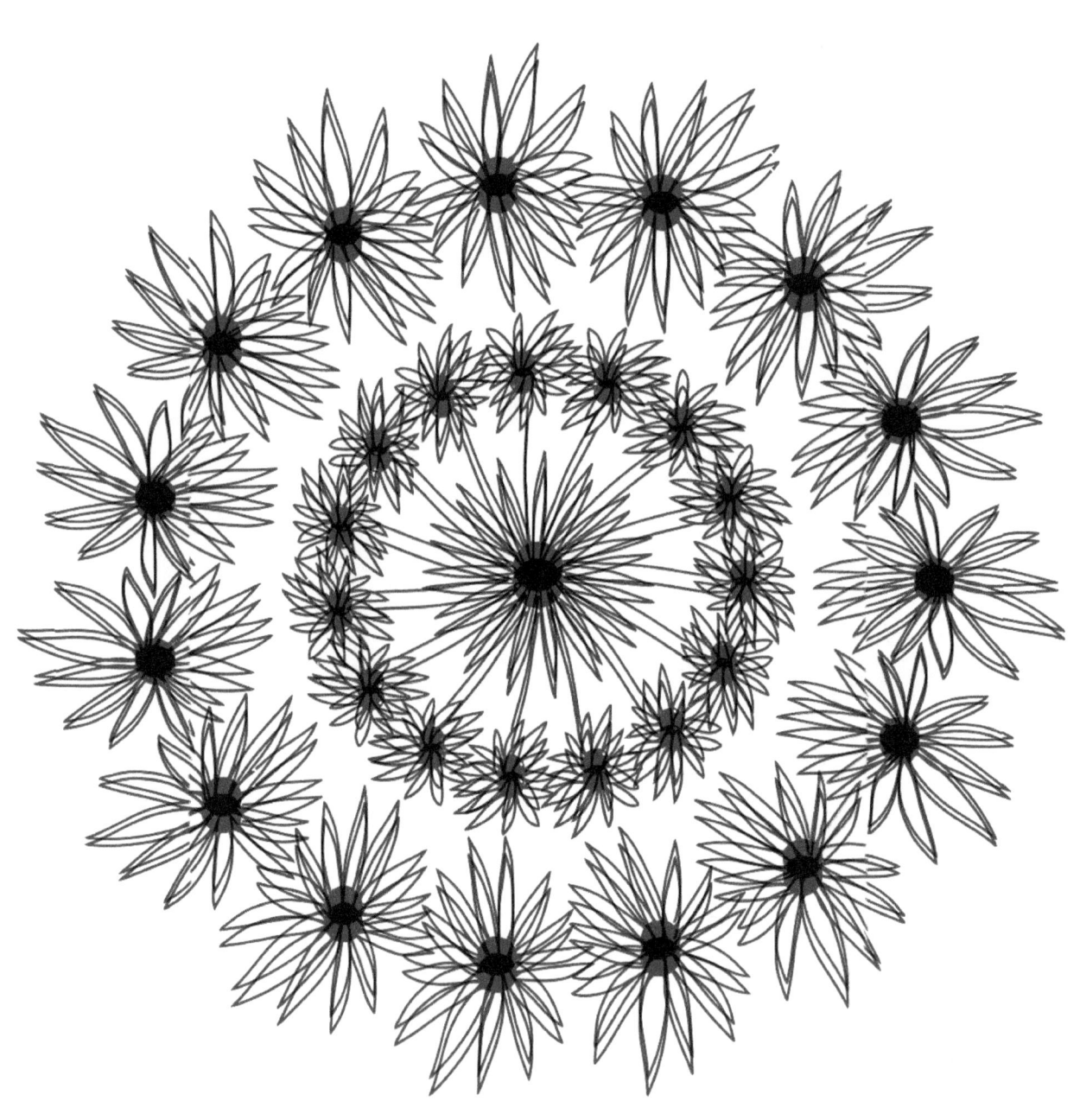

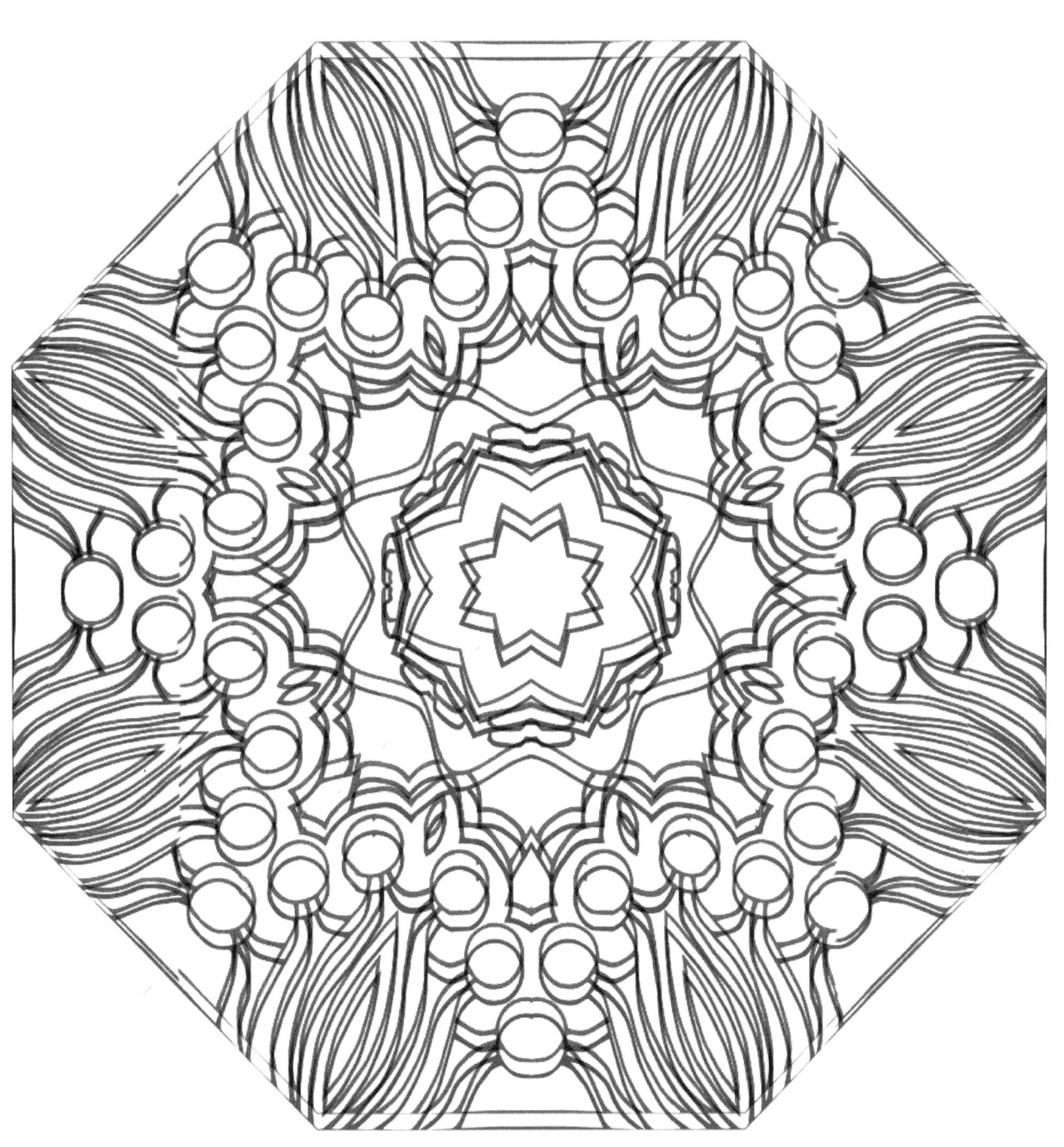

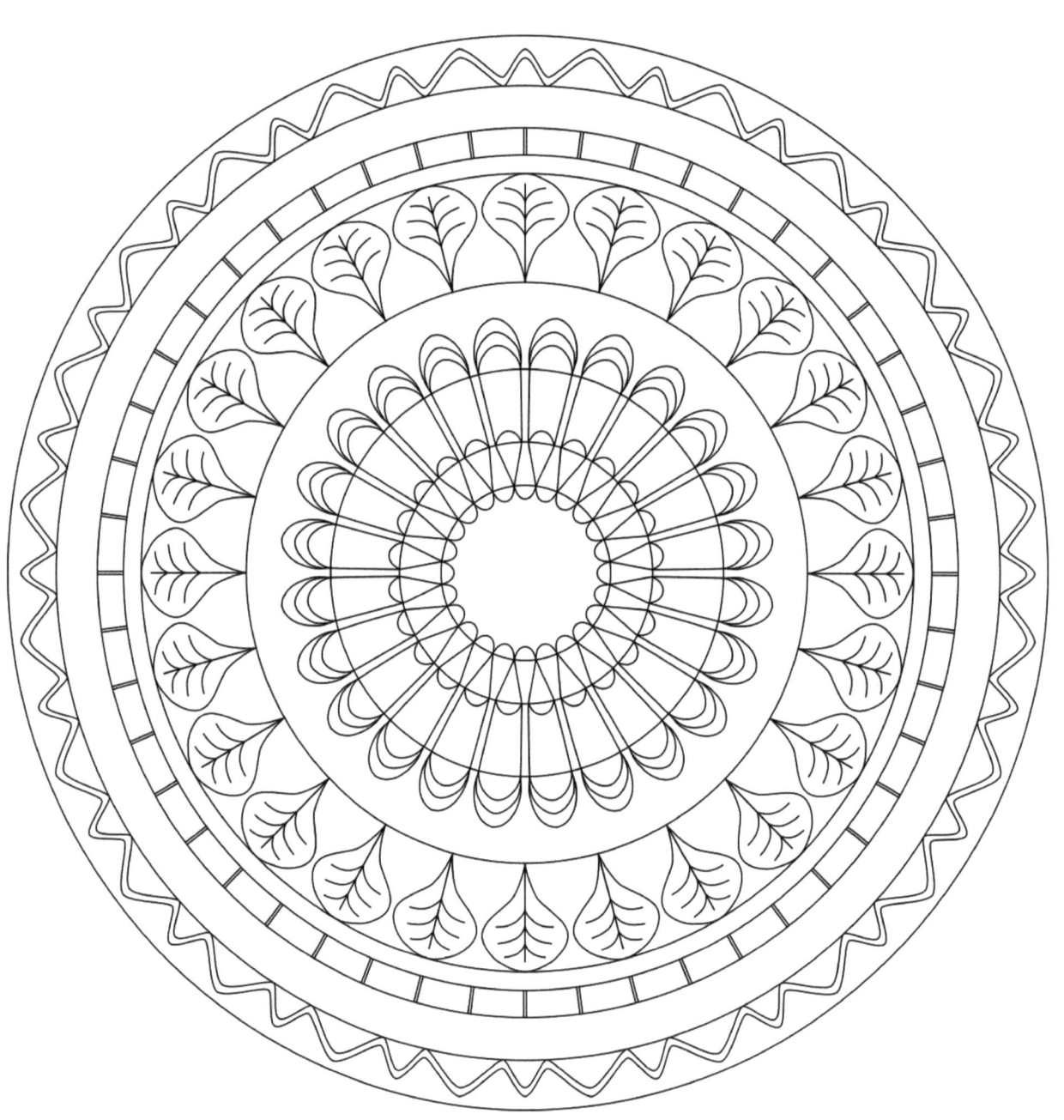

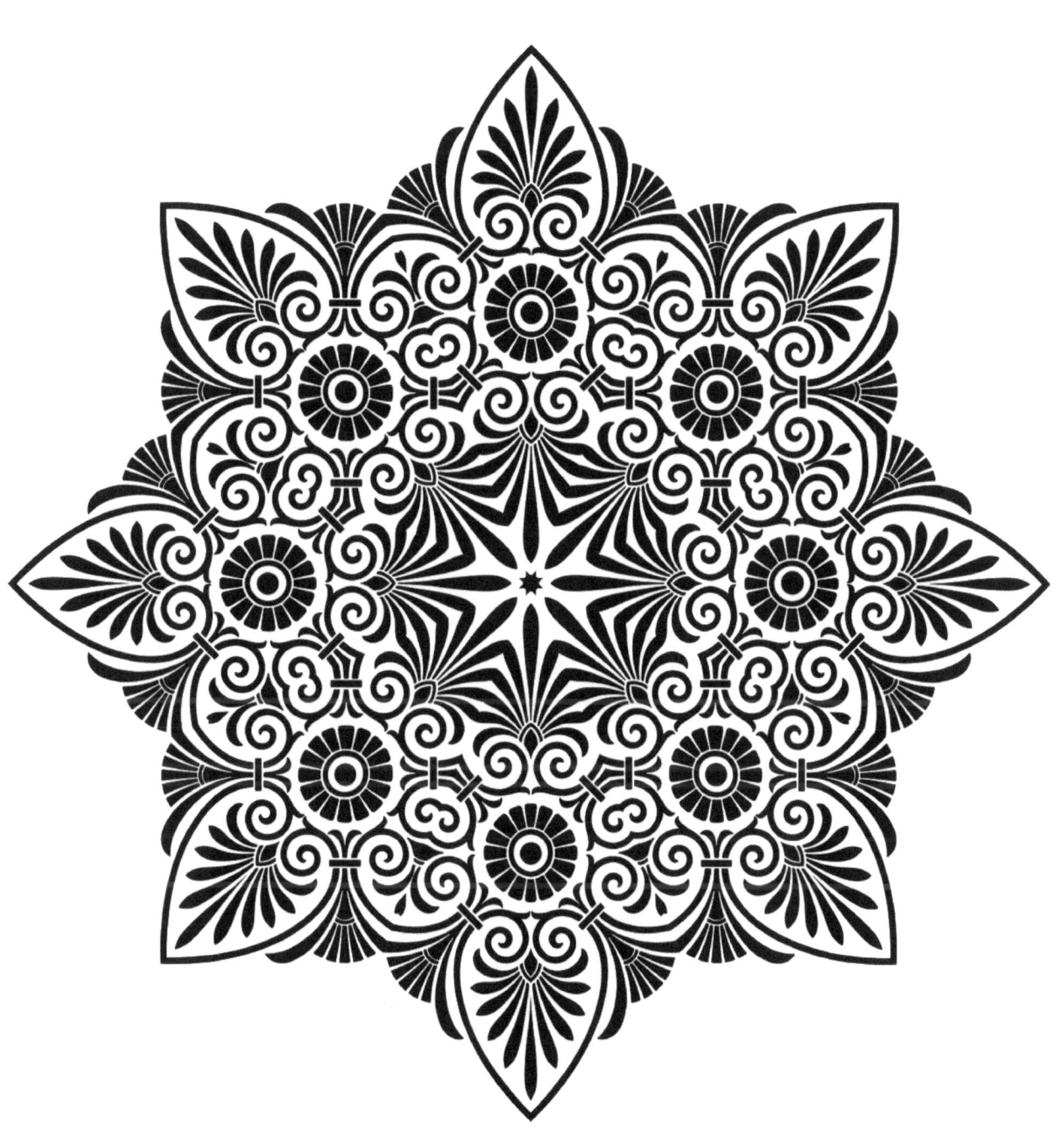

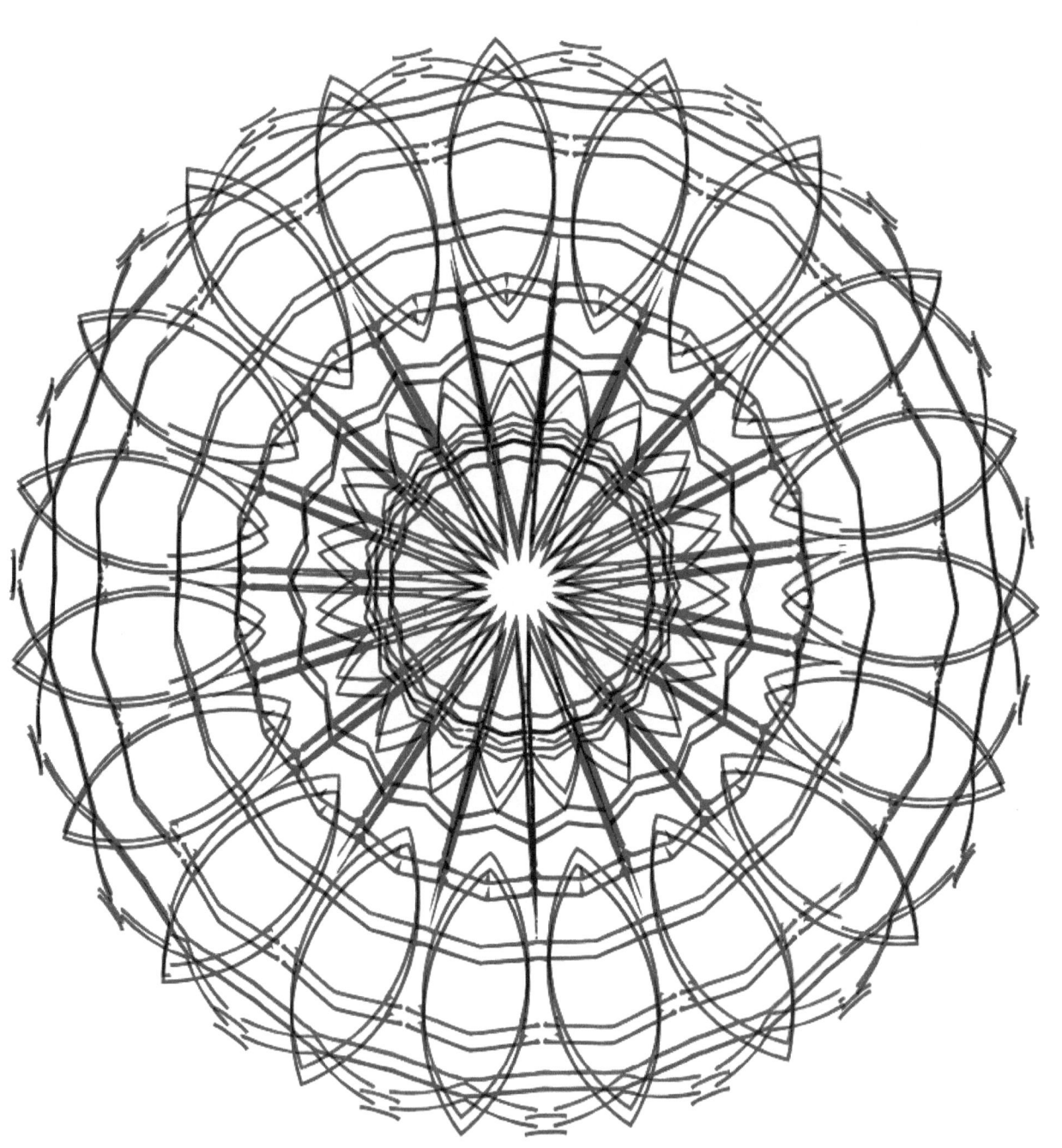

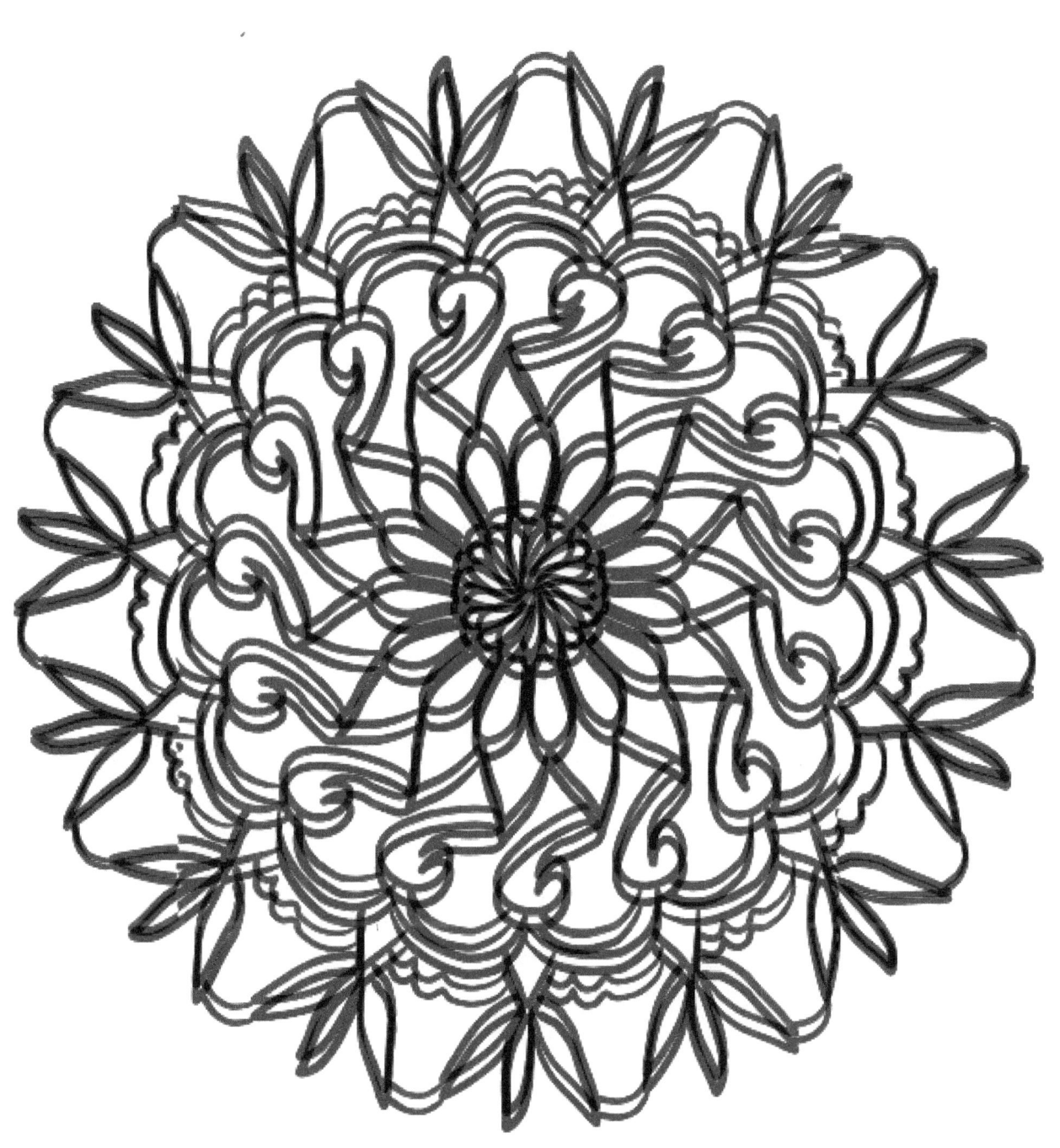

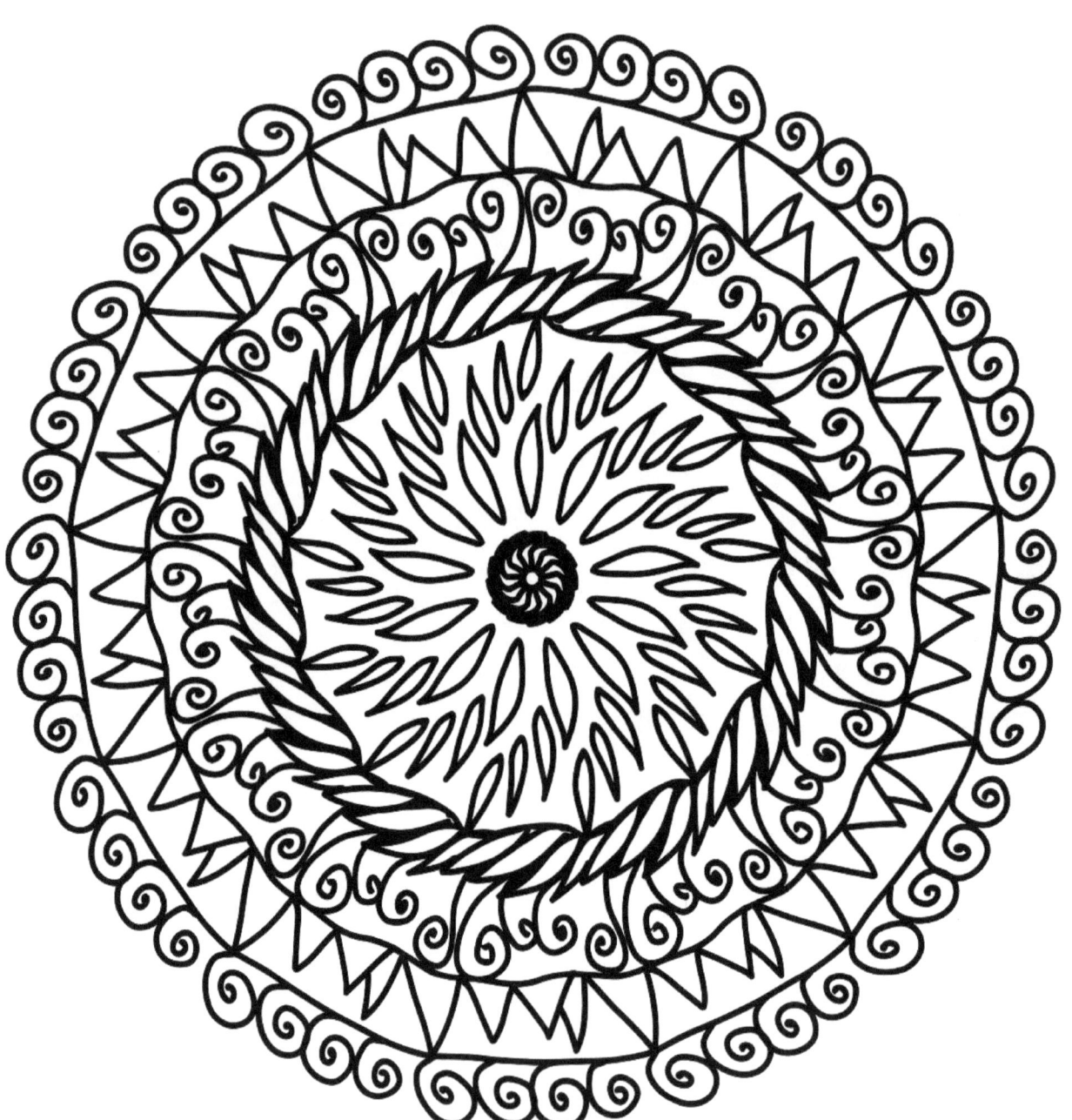